RURAL ACREAGE:

Finding the Right Place

JAMES R. HARRIS

ISBN 0-9637037-0-6

PRINTED ON RECYCLED PAPER BY
ECO-BOOKS
EARTH FRIENDLY BOOK MANUFACTURING
MAVERICK PUBLICATIONS
BEND, OREGON 97701
PRINTED WITH
SOY INK

Printed by
Maverick Publications, Inc.
P.O. Box 5007
Bend, Oregon 97708

Dedicated to Fred Macy, gentleman

Special thanks to:

David Rising
R.W. Eiser
Martin Hall

Rural Acreage: *Finding The Right Place*

TABLE OF CONTENTS

PREFACE

To provide little-known facts and information to the inexperienced land buyer searching for the right place --- from getting that first spark of an idea to actually purchasing a rural parcel --- I have written this informative and practical workbook.

In this guide I uncover many hidden questions and potential obstacles awaiting prospective buyers. The intent is to raise awareness by shedding light on the many facets of purchasing and developing homesite properties.

The worksheets offer you the ability to compare different parcels, using similar guidelines, thus creating accurate assessments and educated decisions.

The illustrations and written details shared are designed to inform while remaining easy to read.

I discuss owning rural land, when and where to buy, real estate transactions, water systems, sewage disposal systems, developing the homesite and access, income production and resale.

I hope you enjoy and find the book to be a valuable asset in your search to *FIND THE RIGHT PLACE.*

James R. Harris

CHAPTER ONE
The Joys Of Owning Rural Land

As the early settlers and pioneers set out across America, their goal was to find land on which to homestead and raise their families: A place to call home. Owning land was the American dream.

Some started this journey in covered wagons, many on horseback, and a few on foot. In the 150 years since, owning land still represents the American dream, but now the situation has changed considerably.

Leaving city life with its services, conveniences and entertainment can be an adventure. Like most adventures, it will have exciting times, difficult obstacles to overcome and moments of wondering if you've made the best decision for you and your family.

People desire to purchase rural acreage for many reasons:

GETTING BACK TO NATURE:

Create your own park
Ability to wander
Create a habitat
Stewardship
Botany and biology
Enjoying nature at home
Gardening
Outdoor hobbies
Geology

RECREATION:

Photography
Hunting
Horseback riding
Fishing
Exploring, walking, jogging
RV trailriding
Bird watching
Tracking

CREATING A LIVELIHOOD:

Farm   Tree Farm

Ranch   Home Business

SPIRITUAL:

Mental well being   Physical health

Slower pace   Sound environment to raise children

Peace and quiet   A positive difference in environment

PERSONAL REASONS:

Self-sufficiency   Raising animals for enjoyment

Controlling your surroundings Security and privacy

Some want to raise their children in a rural environment to avoid negative influences, such as the gangs and high crime rates associated with big city life. Others want to work the land, by farming crops, raising livestock, tree farming or harvesting their own firewood. Some intend to improve the property and later sell for a profit. Others purchase property with intentions to live there after retirement. Many purchase rural property simply for privacy and space.

CHAPTER TWO

When And Where To Buy

Theoretically, the time to buy is now. Today is better than tomorrow, but not as good as yesterday. Since there is only so much land available, it could be described as a limited commodity. Whenever the quantity of a desired item is limited, the cost of that item continues to rise. Generally, the only way to increase the number of parcels of land is to divide existing ownerships into smaller parcels.

Most land use is controlled by governmental bodies such as planning commissions and land-use boards. These bodies use zoning ordinances, comprehensive plans, city, county, state and federal land-use laws to control areas and directions of growth.

Experts have determined that real estate markets follow a cyclical trend. No one knows exactly when the next peak will be or how long it will last. When markets peak it is a *seller's market*, with buyers lined up to buy. Sellers name their price and get it simply because there are more buyers than sellers. When the valley of the cycle comes along it is a *buyer's market*. With many properties available for sale, buyers are able to pick and choose, then make a good buy with good terms. In a buyer's market there are more sellers than buyers. If you have the ability to buy, you have power.

Real estate markets are affected by many factors. Low interest rates and a growing national economy can spur real estate sales. Local growth, as seen in California during the 80's, can send home sales soaring.

People's situations change from time to time and they must sell their property. Divorces prompt the selling of thousands of homes each year. If the existing owner dies, the ownership transfers to the owner's heirs and devisees. These new owners may sell because they do not need the property and desire cash or an income stream generated by the sale. Illness and injury often motivate owners to move to town, closer to medical facilities. Job changes may necessitate property sales. Retirement creates the sale of a home in one area and the purchase of property in another. Thousands of people simply decide to sell their property each year. Foreclosure or threat of foreclosure creates thousands of additional sales each year. Many homes across the country currently for sale are owned by lending institutions. Conditions such as these affect the real estate market, regardless of interest rates or current national economy.

Financial constraints make it difficult for many people who want land to afford it. If you want land when you can afford it, you should start saving now and begin learning about rural acreage in your area. The next time you sit back and say, "Someday I'm going to get a place in the country," you can mean it, if you begin focusing on it now. Whether it be a savings program or learning as much as you can before purchasing a parcel, the time to begin is now.

Many people have sat by and watched neighboring property values go up until they could not afford the property next door. As they watch the parcel sell for $2,000.00 per acre they say, "I remember when I could have bought that for $50.00 per acre." If they had purchased the property then, today they would be the owners of a valuable piece of free and clear land.

If people don't buy because fair market value seems to be too expensive, they are not realizing that in the near future the property may be worth more than the current price. As land owners, you are protecting yourself against future inflation because typically property values go up with inflation, keeping you even. All of these cycles take time and are influenced by local, state, national and worldwide issues. It is a secure feeling to know you have some protection from changes in the economic environment.

If you are a young adult interested in owning land, you have a definite advantage over people your parents' age or older, because you have a longer future. You can afford more time for your property to appreciate. $2,000.00 per acre for a parcel today is the same as $200.00 per acre 25 years ago. I cannot even guess what properties will be worth 25 years from now. They will be precious!

James R. Harris

6

Rural Acreage: *Finding The Right Place*

WHERE TO BUY

Whether staying in your present community or moving to a new area, there are several categories of rural acreage available for consideration: Waterfront, woodland, agricultural, private homesite and investment property.

WATERFRONT

Among homesite properties, those near the ocean, clean rivers or lakes are the most expensive and difficult to find. Historically, waterfront properties continue to appreciate through slumps in the real estate market. The terms of sale are often cash. Because banks do not normally lend money for the purchase of bare land, you must sometimes negotiate terms with the seller.

As areas expand and develop, the availability of homesites along clean rivers reduces until the parcels become a premium. Riverfront properties typically offer irrigation, excellent waterfowl viewing, fishing, boating, swimming, and many other activities that waterless properties simply do not offer. If the parcel is also close to town, it can be of even greater value.

Waterfront properties come in all shapes and sizes. If there are no existing dwellings, you should determine whether or not you can build where you choose. There are high water lines and flood plains to consider. Your real estate agent or County Building Department can assist you.

WOODLAND PROPERTIES

Woodland properties allow their landowners to be actively involved in their management. With the continually rising costs of wood products, wooded properties have potential for future income from tree harvest. It is important to realize how difficult it may be to find parcels with harvestable trees in sufficient numbers to allow the parcel to pay for itself. Usually the seller has already harvested the high volume timber or the asking price reflects the current value of the standing timber.

These acreages, regardless of size, offer more privacy than open parcels. You can often tailor the homesite area to suit particular needs and never see any neighboring homes.

The property may have a mixture of hardwoods, softwoods and open areas. Firs, spruces, pines and cedars are considered softwoods. They are evergreen and maintain foliage throughout the year. Oaks, maples, ashes, alders, dogwoods, birches, fruit and nut trees are examples of hardwoods. They are deciduous, losing their leaves in the fall of the year. Hardwoods on the south-facing side of a home offer solar benefits, as they provide shade in summer and allow the sun to come through in winter.

Fire danger poses the biggest threat of loss to woodland owners. Many times parcels are not part of a fire protection district, resulting in slow response times by local fire fighters. You can, however, minimize the risk of loss or damage by practicing any of several methods to reduce fire danger.

If you are interested in wildlife, wooded parcels allow you to observe wildlife in its own environment. You can improve wildlife habitat and increase the number of species frequenting your property. Wildlife viewing and habitat enhancement have their own rewards. Sometimes the best bird watching is done from your easy chair.

The cost of woodlands varies greatly, depending on the amount of resource (harvestable trees), topography (steepness), location (distance from services and good area versus bad area) and water availability (springs, year-round creeks, seasonal creeks or ponds).

Development costs will include driveway construction, water system, power and telephone installation and septic system. All of these items are essential in preparing for homesite construction.

James R. Harris

AGRICULTURAL

These parcels are generally zoned agriculturally and are specifically used for ranching, farming crops, or as orchards. Once developed they have income-earning capabilities, but require equipment and constant attention. Agricultural lands come in all sizes. You could have two acres with a producing orchard or hundreds of acres of row crops. The best bottom land usually lies next to rivers and brings a higher price.

Ranch lands, or lands best used for raising livestock, also are usually zoned agriculturally.

Purchasing a farm operation is an exciting adventure for the stout of heart. Experience helps. Information on modern, up-to-date farming techniques, proper fence building, feed, seed, etc., is available from county extension agents. For those who enjoy rigorous work and animal husbandry, this is a direction to consider.

HOMESITE PROPERTIES

Rural property does not have to be large to offer the benefits of country living. Depending on location, topography and number of trees, even parcels of one or two acres can offer the owner everything he or she wants.

EXISTING DWELLING

You may be looking for property with a house already on it. If this is the case, many development decisions have already been made for you. Make sure the land and buildings meet your current needs and have the capability to meet your future needs as well. With development and building costs continually rising, buying an already developed property appeals to many prospective purchasers. However, to suit your needs these structures may need modifications requiring substantial improvement costs.

Because sellers' terms are usually cash, transactions involving existing dwellings generally require the buyer to obtain a loan from a bank or other lending institution.

BARE LOTS

Bare lots (no buildings) appeal to many. From retirees to young folks looking ahead, many buyers intend to build later. It is important to note that the buyer should not assume every undeveloped parcel will later be granted a building permit. Make sure the parcel you are interested in qualifies in all necessary respects.

Due to their small sizes, homesite parcels may have limitations concerning home placement. There must be enough room for an approved septic system (including repair area), driveway, home and necessary outbuildings. Be advised that purchasing a parcel without a permit to install an approved septic system could lead to unexpected problems or expense in development.

To build you will need to secure many permits, including permits for such things as a driveway, septic system or sewer hook-up, building, and electrical work.

If you are placing a mobile home, additional permits will be required, including permits for mobile home placement and transportation to your homesite. Your real estate agent or local building department can assist you in this process.

INVESTMENT PROPERTIES

These parcels, generally located in rapidly expanding areas of a growing community, may be divisible, allowing their owners to divide them and resell, unless land-use laws in the area restrict such division. Waterfront properties are often considered to be excellent investment properties. The longer you hold onto these investments, the more valuable they typically

James R. Harris

become.

PRIVACY

One of the biggest attractions of rural acreage is privacy. In cities and even suburbs, homes are so close together that you are looking at a neighbor's house in any direction. Even on small homesite parcels you can usually situate the home for some privacy. Privacy allows you liberty to express yourself, raise your children away from the fast pace of city life or to just enjoy the peace and quiet.

DISTANCE FROM TOWN

If you currently live in an area where long daily commutes to and from work are normal, you may not feel restricted by the distance from your parcel to the nearest population center. However, if you have never commuted, you may not be prepared for ownership of land that is more than 25 miles from town. Before purchasing, you should take into consideration the quality of the roads you will be traveling every day. If retired or not tied to a job, distance from town may mean distance from services such as shopping and medical care. Costs of development and improvements may be higher as distance increases between the parcel and suppliers of sand, gravel, cement and lumber. Your personal situation will determine how much time you are willing to spend commuting.

Keep in mind that parcels become less expensive as they get farther from town. As distance increases between job centers and the parcel, the number of possible buyers decreases. As the ever- growing population expands, these parcels work their way closer to town, becoming more valuable in the process.

ABOUT REAL ESTATE AGENTS

In most states, real estate agents are required to receive a set number of hours of annual education to help keep them abreast of changes in real estate laws and marketing.

Although most real estate agents are hard-working individuals geared to giving you the best service possible, they are not all experts concerning rural acreage. If you are moving to a new area, you don't know if the real estate agent you select will be of the expert variety. It is up to you to know what you are looking for and to ask the right questions.

Real estate agents earn income in the form of commissions paid at time of closing. When salespeople list properties for sale, they secure a portion of the selling commission for their brokers and themselves. Brokers may have several salespersons, each looking for listings, buyers, and, ultimately, sales.

Listing a property with one real estate office does not mean it will not be sold by another. Offices communicate with one another through multiple listing services which give all members the opportunity to sell many of the available properties in their community.

When signing a listing agreement, a potential seller agrees to pay a fee, usually a percentage of the sales price, to the real estate agent upon sale of the property.

For example, you may list a $100,000.00 property in the country and agree to pay a ten percent commission upon closing. If the parcel is sold by a salesperson in another office, the $10,000.00 commission may be split like this:

	LISTING OFFICE:		SELLING OFFICE:	
BROKER:	$2,500.00		BROKER:	$2,500.00
SALESPERSON:	$2,500.00		SALESPERSON:	$2,500.00

This example shows a 50/50 split between listing and selling offices and a 50/50 split between brokers and sales staffs.

Commission splits between offices and between brokers and their salespeople vary. Brokers often offer motivational splits to good salespersons to encourage more sales.

As you can see, if a salesperson sells a property that he or she listed, his or her income would double. If the broker listed and sold the property, the broker would receive 100% of the commission with no salespersons or other offices involved.

Make sure your real estate agent shows you his or her listings as well as all other available listings that might appeal to you.

Sometimes it doesn't take much to muddle a real estate deal. It is the real estate agent's job to satisfy the seller's needs, answer the buyer's questions correctly and keep the deal together. Unfortunately, many proposed sales never close. Real estate agents spend hours running down loose ends while trying to keep buyers and sellers happy. When a sale fails, the real estate agent doesn't earn a penny.

A conscientious real estate agent can be very helpful in finding a place because he or she can show you most of the properties available in the area, and tell you which areas are best and why.

FOR SALE BY OWNER

For-sale-by-owner properties, called *FISBO's* by some in the industry, can be found by looking in the real estate classified section of the local newspaper. Real estate agents do not always have access to these parcels because the owners want to sell their properties without using the services of a real estate agent. Many times you are on your own running down privately advertised parcels.

CHAPTER THREE

What Really Happens In A Real Estate Transaction

Paying cash for property is the quickest and simplest way to get past financing hurdles. Only a few buyers pay cash, with most having to finance their purchases.

Remember, banks do not normally lend money to purchase bare land. Many deals fail because buyers cannot secure financing that they presumed was available.

To start, figure out how much you can afford to pay down on a parcel, and then how much you can safely pay each month thereafter.

If a parcel has a house on it, the bank may lend a large percentage of its value, but you must come up with the other remainder plus the price of the land itself for a down payment. Sometimes banks allow the down payment to be borrowed. Money for down payments sometimes comes from family loans, employer pension-fund loans, cash value of life insurance policies, refinancing other property, selling other property, or savings programs.

Lending institutions vary in lending policies. Land banks and lending co-operatives are geared to loan money on ranch and farmland and use livestock, crops, buildings, equipment and land as collateral. Banks will finance new construction, but the land must typically be free and clear. When a bank prepares a loan, it sends an appraiser out to establish a value for the existing dwelling. The appraiser also notes anything that would make the house non-financible, such as no foundation, leaky roof, settling damage, faulty plumbing or obvious abuse. The bank then decides how much money will be loaned toward the purchase of the home.

Conventional loans come with names like *trust deeds, deeds of trust or mortgages*. The differences between these are in the terms of foreclosure and are of little concern to most buyers.

You can sit down with a friendly banker for one hour and afterward know how much money the bank will lend toward a new home based on your ability to repay. YOU NEED TO

KNOW WHAT YOU CAN AFFORD BEFORE YOU TRY TO BUY.

Mortgage brokers often have investors willing to lend money on bare land. You may be able to borrow a reasonable percentage of the land's value, but the interest rate will be higher than a bank's. Mortgage brokers are one of very few places to borrow money on small parcels of bare land.

If your seller is interested in a flow of income over several years rather than cash, he or she may be willing to finance the purchase.

Land sale contracts or contracts of sale are forms of installment sales. You make a down payment, then monthly payments to the seller until payoff. You then receive and record the deed. These contracts can be written with almost any terms that are agreeable to both buyer and seller. Trust deeds or mortgages can also be used in seller-financed installment sales. Either you or the seller, or both of you may want to use the services of an attorney to prepare the sale documents. Most bare land is sold through some form of owner-financed installment sale. Ads in the newspaper's classified section may say, "Owner Financing Available."

DEALING WITH THE SELLER

If buying through a real estate agent, your conversations with the seller may be limited. You may never even meet the seller. A good real estate agent will be able to answer all of the following questions about each parcel:

> How much are the annual taxes?
> Are there any tax exemptions?
> Are there any easements across this property?
> Is this property dependent on easements of any kind
> across neighboring parcels?
> Are there any protective covenants?

Where is the septic system or the approved site? Show me.

Where are the property corners? Show me.

Where does the water come from? Show me.

Where do power and telephone lines come from? Show me.

How is this property zoned?

How are the neighbors?

Is the property fenced?

In what condition is the fence?

Can this parcel be divided?**

Can two dwellings be legally put on the property?**

What are projected future uses for neighboring parcels?**

     (A proposed shopping center, airport, or land fill

     nearby may affect your decision to purchase.)

    ** You may prefer to research these three questions for yourself, without asking the owner.

When dealing with the seller directly you will need to ask these questions to protect yourself. The seller may or may not be able to answer these questions. Many sellers do not know how their property is zoned, or whether it can be legally divided. Having more than one dwelling constructed on the property is probably a question you will need to check out for certain. This means you may have some legwork to do at the county courthouse. Questions concerning zoning and land use can be answered by the County Planning Department.

AGREEMENT TO PURCHASE

When all your questions have been answered and you have decided to buy the parcel, you must come to terms with the seller. After agreeing on terms, you and the seller prepare an *earnest money agreement.* Earnest money is usually $100.00 to $5,000.00 and represents that you are earnest about purchasing the property. If the transaction fails, earnest monies usually go to the seller. Buyers must be willing to lose this earnest money if failing to meet the terms of the earnest money agreement.

In filling out the earnest money receipt, you and the seller tentatively agree on terms that may last several years. The earnest money receipt is easily filled out by carefully reading every word and filling in the blanks. When the agreement is signed by both parties it is ready to go to the title insurance company. Earnest money agreement forms are available at local stationery stores or any business that sells legal forms. Some title companies offer these forms free of charge.

TITLE INSURANCE COMPANIES

A title company is an important part of any real estate transaction. Upon receiving a copy of the earnest money receipt and the earnest monies, the title company prepares and issues a preliminary title report. This report shows the vestee (owner), proper legal description, evidence of any easements that cross the parcel, mortgages, trust deeds, contracts of sale and liens or judgments against the seller. If the report is for a lender it will also show the result of a judgment search of the buyers. When the report is finished, it is sent to the buyer and seller or the real estate agents. You may wish to have your attorney receive a copy as well.

As a buyer it is important for you to read the preliminary title report because it discloses all clouds of record (things that could adversely affect your interest in the property) against the property you are buying. Make sure these exceptions are acceptable to you. Have them explained if you do not understand.

Most title companies also offer two escrow services; one is for closing escrowed transactions and the other is for collecting payments to be made after the sale has been closed.

James R. Harris

CLOSING ESCROWS

In a closing escrow the escrow agent (title company, attorney or private escrow company) acts as a third party for the benefit of both buyer and seller. The escrow agent assembles needed documents, prorates taxes, gets pay-off figures for existing liens or judgments that are to be satisfied prior to closing and prepares a detailed closing statement showing how each dollar has been spent during the transaction.

When the buyer's money comes into the title company and all instruments (documents) have been properly signed, assembled and recorded, the escrow agent uses the buyer's money to satisfy unpaid taxes, contracts of sale, trust deeds, mortgages and judgments that need to be satisfied prior to closing. The escrow agent also pays the real estate commission, attorney fees and county recording fees. This process may take several days, during which time you are welcome to call and check on your transaction's progress. Once the title is in the condition you agreed to purchase, the agent will record all necessary instruments, making your interest a matter of public record.

In most states the seller pays for and provides title insurance to the buyer. The buyer may be responsible for paying one-half the closing escrow fee, proration of pre-paid taxes, attorney fees and recording fees. If you are using a lending institution, you will have to provide the lender with a mortgagee's policy of title insurance.

COLLECTION ESCROWS

If the seller is financing the purchase, you probably signed collection escrow instructions during closing. Collection escrow service allows you to make your monthly payment to the escrow agent.

In a contract sale the agent holds the deed with instructions to record it upon pay-off, sometimes years later. As the buyer's payments come in, the agent disburses the funds to the seller. In another type of installment sale, the escrow agent collects payments until the balance is paid in full, at which time the agent sends documents to the buyer to satisfy the seller's interest upon final payment.

Collection escrow services can be found at title insurance companies, banks and private escrow companies. Collection escrows are considered more advantageous to the purchaser than paying directly to an individual seller, as this way the purchaser knows that he or she will receive documents to properly clear the property of the seller's interest in the property.

CLOSING COSTS

When people mention closing costs, they are referring to the costs that arise during the closing escrow. Closing costs typically paid by the seller include title insurance, one-half of the closing escrow fee, tax proration, real estate commission, county recording fees, satisfaction of any liens not acceptable to the buyer, and attorney fees.

For the seller, knowing what these costs are will help determine how much money must be obtained as a down payment to meet closing costs and personal needs. All or most of the seller's costs will be paid with the purchaser's down payment monies during closing escrow. Closing costs typically paid by the buyer include one-half of the closing escrow fee, tax proration, county recording fees, bank charges (loan fee, credit report fee, etc.) and attorney fees.

To the buyer, these closing costs show how much additional money will be added to the purchase price to cover closing costs.

An example of a typical sale: Mr. Jones has a 50-acre parcel with an established value of $100,000.00. He has decided to sell, and his real estate agent has connected him with the buyer, Mr. Smith. Through the real estate agent, Mr. Jones and Mr. Smith have entered into an earnest money agreement including the following terms: Buyer is to deposit $2,000.00 as earnest money; buyer is to make a $30,000.00 down payment into the closing escrow after approving conditions of the title as set out by the preliminary title report; buyer is to make payments of $1,000.00 per month including interest on the unpaid balance until it is paid in full; seller is to provide a purchaser's title insurance policy for buyer; seller and buyer are to split closing escrow fees; seller and buyer to are split collection escrow setup fees; seller and buyer are to split attorney fees for preparation of installment sale documents; seller is to pay real estate commission of $10,000.00.

Mr. Jones has the following expenses:

Real estate commission	$10,000.00
Closing Costs	$1,500.00
Cash needs from sale	$20,500.00
Total	$32,000.00

Mr. Jones knew the minimum down payment acceptable was $30,000.00 plus $2,000.00 earnest money.

The earnest money agreement is signed and delivered to the title company, escrow agent and attorney. The $2,000.00 earnest money is put into the closing escrow at this time.

The title company will produce a preliminary title report showing the date of the report, vestee (legal owner), exact legal description, easements or rights-of-way that cross the parcel, mortgages, deeds of trust, land sale contracts, any lien for money that has been recorded against the parcel and not yet satisfied, assignments, agreements, anything recorded against the parcel that creates a cloud on the title, and any liens for money against the seller personally that attach to the property (such as unpaid child support, attorney liens, tax liens, and judgments recorded in courts of equity).

Although the services of an attorney may prove beneficial in preparing sale documents, it should be noted that as a buyer or seller you are not required to use these services.

After receiving the preliminary title report, Mr Smith can see that there are no problems with the Jones parcel. The attorney of choice also receives the preliminary report and begins to prepare documents for the installment sale, using his copy of the earnest money agreement to understand the terms of sale.

Upon receiving finished documents (instruments), the escrow agent asks the buyer and seller to come in and sign all papers. Once the instruments are signed and notarized, the escrow agent will record evidence of the installment sale. When recording is complete, the escrow agent will disburse monies as follows:

Real estate commission	$10,000.00
Title insurance policy	$500.00
Closing escrow fee	$400.00
Unpaid taxes to date of closing	$450.00
Collection escrow setup fee	$100.00
Attorney fee	$500.00
Recording fees	$50.00
Mr. Jones	$20,500.00
TOTAL	$32,500.00

In this example, Mr. Smith, the buyer, must come up with the following closing costs, in addition to his down payment:

One-half closing escrow fee	$200.00
One-half of escrow setup fee	$50.00
One-half of attorney fee	$250.00
TOTAL	$500.00

(Buyers must sometimes pay recording fees and a prorated share of any prepaid real estate taxes as part of their closing costs.)

During closing, the collection escrow was set up, and the signed (but unrecorded) deed was placed in a vault, ready to be recorded upon final pay-off by the new owner. The new owner makes a $1,000.00 monthly payment to the escrow agent, perhaps never again to have contact with the previous owner. The escrow agent forwards the payment to the seller after computing principal and interest.

After closing (recording of instruments and disbursing of monies), Mr. Smith, now the owner, has the right to enjoy his new property.

CHAPTER FOUR
Water And Water Systems

Availability of water is among the most important considerations when shopping for rural property. Ample water will enhance the pleasures of ownership, not to mention resale potential. Parcels with little or no water potential can be difficult to sell. When looking at properties during the wet season, it is difficult to assess the availability of water at the peak of the dry season. Long dry summers with very little water can stress the thrill of ownership.

There are many different ways in which water is manifest, including rivers, seasonal creeks, streams, wetlands, lakes, wells, ponds, water districts and springs.

RIVERS

Rivers with large volumes of water typically offer year-round irrigation and domestic usage. Once the proper permits are secured, you can legally use a specified volume for authorized purposes. Securing water rights can be accomplished at the nearest state water resource authority's office. Acquiring water rights is not always a simple matter, and involves paper work, red tape and fees.

River-based water systems can be difficult to install and have a history of high maintenance. Rising water levels and the ever-changing river bottom make it difficult to predict the reaction caused by installing an intake pump. The adjoining land owners may aid in suggesting what type of installation works for that portion of the river. With cloudy winter water and up-river unknowns, purification and filtering peripherals are a must for a river system.

When taking domestic water (water used for household purposes) from a river, the pump station must be built in such a way as to survive flooding. This can be difficult and expensive. Owners usually develop an alternate source for domestic water and use the river for irrigation only.

Irrigation pumps are generally removed from rivers in the fall to avoid damage from flooding and re-installed the following spring.

Excellent water availability and existing water rights add to the value of riverfront properties. With virtually unlimited irrigation water, the owner has a wide array of options for developmental or agricultural pursuits.

Generally, the older the water rights, the better. As water flows reduce during the summer's heat, the state water resource authority may have to shut down several users. This is typically accomplished by contacting owners with the most recent water rights and ordering them to stop pumping from the river for irrigation purposes. In some areas late summer flows affect all but the oldest water rights. Whenever looking at property with flowing water, ask the seller if there are water rights and what the priority of the rights may be. If you get more serious about this property, examine the water right certificates BEFORE CLOSING.

Most states do not allow home construction within boundaries of the floodplain. Floodplains are normally dry land that becomes submerged during flooding. These boundary lines may represent water levels during a one-hundred-year flood; i.e., the highest point the water has reached in the last 100 years. The location of the floodplain can make a big value difference on small, riverfront parcels.

LAKES

In some areas, lakefront properties are the most desired homesite parcels. Other lakefront areas cater to summer and vacation homesites. There are also lakes on private land.

Your potential use will depend on water use regulations in the area. If there is municipal or water-district water available, you may not be allowed to take water from the lake. When allowed to develop a domestic water system, lake water must typically be purified to meet domestic water standards.

Because lake levels are usually more stable than river levels, home construction may be allowed very near the water's edge. Make sure to answer all your water-related questions and examine existing water rights, if any, BEFORE CLOSING.

STREAMS

Properties with a year-round creek usually command a higher price than those properties without flowing water. Flowing throughout the dry months of summer, these waterways are beneficial to wildlife and livestock. Livestock, however, can destroy streamsides quickly if not managed.

Year-round streams offer the potential to irrigate for agricultural purposes, livestock watering or gardening. The state water resource authority, however, may restrict pumping by some of the more recently-acquired water rights during times of low-stream flow.

It is possible to develop a domestic water intake system on a year-round stream after acquiring domestic use water rights from the state water resource authority and have ample water for household use. Because of lower flows, water intake systems on small streams may be easier to maintain than those systems on larger rivers.

If you are interested in wildlife, the presence of water assures you the highest potential for successful habitat development. In many cases, there is great potential for increasing the property's value by improving riparian zones. IN THIS AGE OF ENVIRONMENTAL AWARENESS, MORE AND MORE PEOPLE ARE BUYING PROPERTY WITH WILDLIFE VIEWING AS ONE OF THEIR CONSIDERATIONS.

Just like the early settlers, many people feel having a year-round stream makes their property complete. THE POTENTIAL FOR SELF SUFFICIENCY IS GREATLY ENHANCED BY YEAR-ROUND, FLOWING WATER.

SEASONAL CREEKS

Seasonal creeks do not flow during the dry part of the year. If looking at property for the first time, and it's winter, you may get the impression that the creek runs all year. As you get more serious about this parcel, ask neighbors if the creek runs all year and how much flow there is in late summer. Water rights can be an important issue. You should determine that whatever water there is may not be controlled by an upstream or downstream owner.

Parcels with seasonal creeks are usually less expensive than parcels with year-round, flowing water and more expensive than parcels with no flowing water at all.

SPRINGS

A spring could be described as a source of water issuing from the ground. Springs are typically found flowing from fractured rock or lie just under ground surface, creating a wet spot or year-round green area.

With proper development, a good spring can give the owner the benefits of limited irrigation.

Springs normally flow water 24 hours per day. Thus, what may appear as a small volume may provide ample water for daily domestic use. One gallon of water per minute will produce 1,440 gallons per day. Collecting and containing as much water as possible may make the difference between having or not having enough.

Illustration 4-1 shows water originating from fractured rock. The water is collected by way of a small dam. Water is then distributed to a pump vault ready for pumping to the home site. Pump vaults are used to collect water 24 hours per day and hold enough water for each normal pumping cycle. Switches and devices may be needed to accomplish this. Each system includes an overflow to insure all excess water flows away from development areas, thereby reducing erosion. These excess overflows can be utilized to water livestock or wildlife. A

SURFACE TYPE
SPRING DEVELOPMENT

ILLUSTRATION 4-1

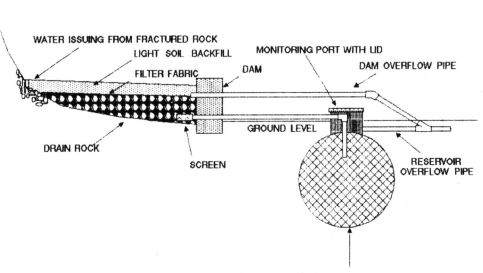

WATER ISSUING FROM FRACTURED ROCK

LIGHT SOIL BACKFILL

FILTER FABRIC

DAM

MONITORING PORT WITH LID

DAM OVERFLOW PIPE

DRAIN ROCK

SCREEN

GROUND LEVEL

RESERVOIR
OVERFLOW PIPE

PUMP VAULT FOR PUMPING TO STORAGE TANK

OR

PLACE STORAGE TANK HERE IF ROOM PERMITS
THEN PUMP OR GRAVITY FEED TO HOMESITE

sturdy fence will prohibit access and limit animal damage and contamination.

If, after development, the spring produces low volume, a storage tank should be added to the system. This storage tank will decrease the possibility of running short of water during the dry season. In many cases a sealed 1,500-gallon concrete tank will prove adequate.

There are various ways to include a storage tank in a spring development. If the flow into the tank is continuous, an overflow will be required. The continuous flow to the tank can be regulated by a mechanical float valve in a gravity system. In a pumping system, a mercury-type float switch controls the level in the tank by switching the pump on and off. Illustration 4-2 shows three different applications of storage tank usage.

Suitable water close to the surface may allow a simple and cost-effective shallow well development, as shown in Illustration 4-3. Illustration 4-4 shows a shallow well constructed on the inside bend of a stream. This system is dependable and not difficult to install. Because the water flows through stream-bed gravel, it remains clear and resistant to clouding, making this system more desirable than an in-stream system. In-stream systems may be subjected to great forces of water during flooding.

Water rights concerning springs are very important. If existing water rights are held by the seller, be sure these rights are conveyed to you. If the spring is one of the reasons you have decided to buy the parcel, you should determine who has the legal right to use its water.

WELLS

Wells are drilled underground to reach a source of water, then encased with pipe to prevent any slumping. A submersible pump is lowered into the water to provide water to the property. How much water a new well will produce is a guessing game at best, and some areas have a reputation for *dry holes*.

The cost of drilling a well is primarily based on the depth of the hole. Talk to adjoining land owners and check the well records at the state water resource authority's office to determine

TYPICAL SYSTEMS

ILLUSTRATION 4-2

PUMPING INTO STORAGE TANK
PUMPING OUT OF STORAGE TANK

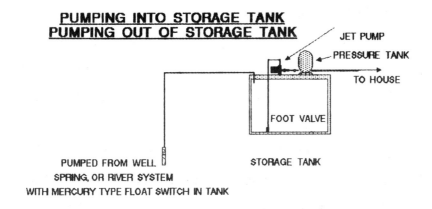

JET PUMP

PRESSURE TANK

TO HOUSE

FOOT VALVE

PUMPED FROM WELL
SPRING, OR RIVER SYSTEM
WITH MERCURY TYPE FLOAT SWITCH IN TANK

STORAGE TANK

GRAVITY INTO STORAGE TANK
PUMPING OUT OF STORAGE TANK

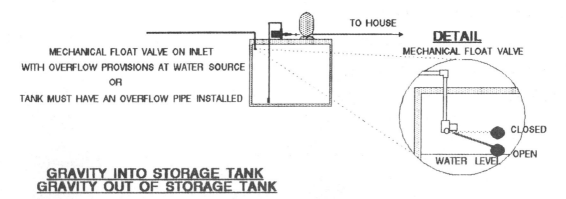

TO HOUSE

DETAIL

MECHANICAL FLOAT VALVE ON INLET
WITH OVERFLOW PROVISIONS AT WATER SOURCE
OR
TANK MUST HAVE AN OVERFLOW PIPE INSTALLED

MECHANICAL FLOAT VALVE

CLOSED

OPEN

WATER LEVEL

GRAVITY INTO STORAGE TANK
GRAVITY OUT OF STORAGE TANK

SPRING FED TO STORAGE TANK AT THE RATE OF 1 GALLON PER MINUTE
WILL COLLECT 1440 GALLONS OF WATER IN A 24 HR PERIOD
A SPRING THAT PRODUCES 1 GALLON OF WATER EVERY 3 MINUTES
WILL COLLECT 480 GALLONS IN A 24 HOUR PERIOD

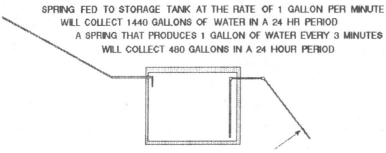

GRAVITY FLOW TO HOUSE ON DEMAND

AVERAGE HOUSEHOLD USAGE PER DAY IS LESS THAN 480 GALLONS OF WATER

SHALLOW WELL DEVELOPMENTS

ILLUSTRATION 4-3

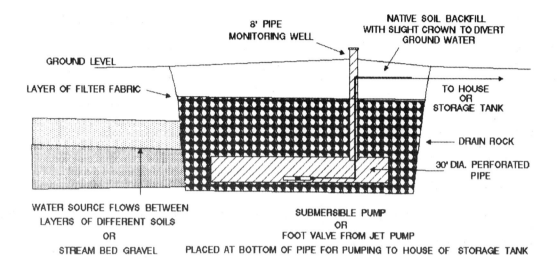

8' PIPE
MONITORING WELL

NATIVE SOIL BACKFILL
WITH SLIGHT CROWN TO DIVERT
GROUND WATER

GROUND LEVEL

LAYER OF FILTER FABRIC

TO HOUSE
OR
STORAGE TANK

DRAIN ROCK

30' DIA. PERFORATED
PIPE

WATER SOURCE FLOWS BETWEEN
LAYERS OF DIFFERENT SOILS
OR
STREAM BED GRAVEL

SUBMERSIBLE PUMP
OR
FOOT VALVE FROM JET PUMP
PLACED AT BOTTOM OF PIPE FOR PUMPING TO HOUSE OF STORAGE TANK

ILLUSTRATION 4-4

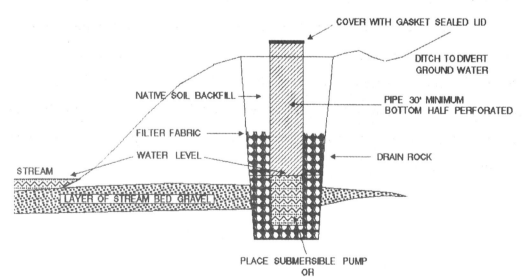

COVER WITH GASKET SEALED LID

DITCH TO DIVERT
GROUND WATER

NATIVE SOIL BACKFILL

PIPE 30' MINIMUM
BOTTOM HALF PERFORATED

FILTER FABRIC

WATER LEVEL

DRAIN ROCK

STREAM

LAYER OF STREAM BED GRAVEL

PLACE SUBMERSIBLE PUMP
OR
FOOT VALVE FROM JET PUMP AT BOTTOM OF 30" PIPE
FOR PUMPING TO STORAGE TANK OR HOUSE

depth, volume and quality of wells in the area.

Unfortunately, not all well water is *potable*, or safe to drink. High concentrations of minerals such as salt or sulphur are undesirable but possibly remedied through filtration and purification systems. With improving technology, even the most undesirable water may be made suitable.

Most sellers know that selling property with the water potential already developed commands a higher price than property without water development. When it comes to water, many buyers refuse to gamble on its presence. They would rather continue looking for a parcel they know has water. Some sellers have drilled dry wells during their ownership and are selling because of lack of water. These parcels may be less expensive, but hauling water can certainly take some enjoyment out of property ownership.

Wells that produce in excess of six gallons of potable water per minute in late summer will typically give the owner satisfactory volume for most uses. With proper storage facilities you can have ample water with lower volumes.

PONDS

Ponds on property offer beauty, irrigation possibilities, livestock watering and water for wildlife, but they do not normally offer water for domestic use. Because pond water, referred to as *surface water*, is exposed to the elements and animals of all types, it contains bacteria not acceptable for human consumption. In many states ponds require permits from the state water resource authority. Make sure you are comfortable with the status of the pond before closing. Once you have established another source for domestic water, a good spring-fed pond offers many benefits to your property.

WATER DISTRICTS

Water districts provide water to many rural parcels around developed communities. Although this water is expensive, the availability of water provided by a water district reduces your obligation to drill a well or develop a marginal spring. If a parcel lies within the service area of a water district, it is saleable without the visible presence of water.

When applying for water at your water district, it may be required that membership or stock in the organization be purchased. There could also be hook-up or connection fees, plus excavation and installation charges.

WETLANDS

As government regulations continue to stiffen, wetlands may all be subject to governmental control in the near future. A *no-net-loss* wetland policy means you can do very little, if anything, to an existing wetland without proper governmental authorization. Keep this in mind if you want to construct your new home on the edge of an existing marsh, pond or estuary.

Wetlands offer some of the best wildlife watching available. Whether migrating waterfowl or local-resident wildlife, many animals are attracted to the food, shelter, and water the wetland provides. A healthy wetland area is an attribute to any property.

CHAPTER FIVE

On-Site Sewage Disposal Systems

One of the most important considerations in selecting a parcel is septic system approval.

Approval or denial of a septic system is primarily determined by soil composition of the area in which the system is to be installed. Another factor is location of the system in relation to wells, rivers, intermittent streams, ponds and other water sources. Additional limitations are property lines, easements, roadways, escarpments, man-made cuts and building set-back requirements. Illustration 5-1 describes how some of these setbacks influence septic system placement.

Soil conditions ultimately determine the type of system to be installed. Costs of these systems vary greatly. As a purchaser, you should know which type of system is required on the parcel you are considering. This allows accurate assessment of development costs for the parcel. One parcel could cost $3,000.00 less, but may require a septic system costing an additional $7,000.00 to install. Perhaps the approved septic system area occupies the most obvious building site, forcing you to select a more difficult homesite, ultimately increasing development costs.

An on-site evaluation will determine the type of system needed, including specifications and location of the initial and repair areas. Typically there must be enough area available to construct the initial system plus a repair system for future use to obtain an approval. If the parcel does not have a site evaluation, request the real estate agent or seller to provide one.

The county building department can assist in determining the agency which governs septic system installations. Generally, this agency cannot recommend a particular septic system installer, but can provide a list of licensed installers in that county. When dealing with installers, ask questions and check references.

James R. Harris

SITE PLAN USING SET BACKS

ILLUSTRATION 5-1

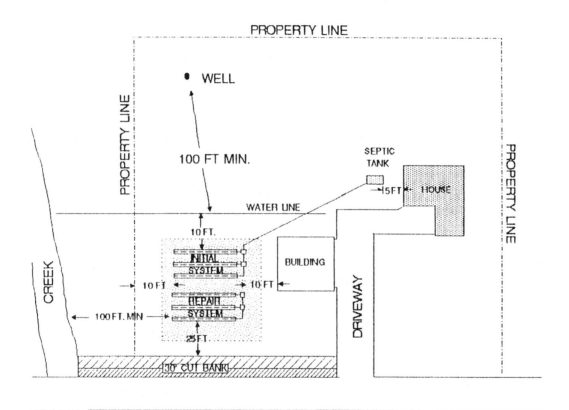

ALL SET BACKS ARE MINIMUM DISTANCES

APPROVAL AREA

A few standard questions to ask any installer you are considering include:

> Can you build the system the permit requires?
>
> Have you installed this type of system before?
>
> > If so, how many?
>
> What type of tank will be installed?
>
> > Concrete/fiberglass/plastic/metal?
>
> When can you start?
>
> How long will it take?
>
> Do you have insurance and a performance bond?

A contractor should be able to provide proof of insurance at your request. If the contractor is not licensed and bonded, liability could fall to the land owner in the event of injury or accident.

The following examples and illustrations describe commonly used systems for on-site sewage disposal.

STANDARD SYSTEMS

Standard systems are gravity-fed, inexpensive and the least difficult to install. They consist of a septic tank and disposal field, or drain field.

Septic tanks are water-tight receptacles that receive sewage, separate solids from liquids and digest organic matter, thereby allowing liquids to discharge into the disposal field.

The disposal field is a series of level trenches with pipe and drain rock. However, these trenches may be on different elevations based on the topography of the approved site. Length of disposal field is also determined by soil conditions. Illustration 5-2 shows a cross section of a typical drain field.

DISPOSAL FIELD CROSS-SECTION

STANDARD TRENCH

ILLUSTRATION 5-2

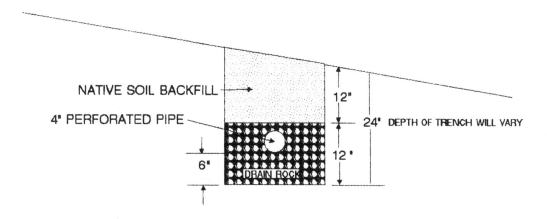

NATIVE SOIL BACKFILL

4" PERFORATED PIPE

12"

24" DEPTH OF TRENCH WILL VARY

12"

6"

DRAIN ROCK

CAPPING FILL

ILLUSTRATION 5-3

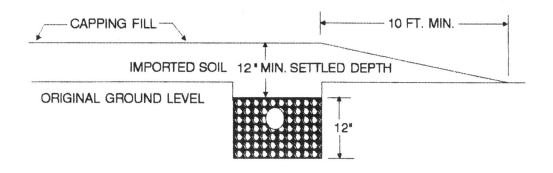

CAPPING FILL

10 FT. MIN.

IMPORTED SOIL 12" MIN. SETTLED DEPTH

ORIGINAL GROUND LEVEL

12"

CAPPING FILL SYSTEMS

A capping fill system is a shallow disposal field covered with imported soil. See Illustration 5-3. Capping soils must be inspected for texture and moisture content prior to construction of the cap. This soil can be borrowed from another area away from the disposal and repair areas. When approved, capping soil must be hauled in from a distant source, and the system can become costly.

PUMPING SYSTEMS

In some cases the approved area for the drain field is uphill from the proposed building site. Whether the elevation increases one inch or one hundred feet, you will need to pump effluent to the disposal field. The addition of a pump is not a major obstacle, but it will add the cost of the pump itself, switches, alarms, control panels and electricity to the cost of the overall septic system.

CURTAIN DRAINS

Depending on site conditions, a curtain drain may be required as an integral part of the complete septic system. This is a trench filled with drain rock with perforated pipe at the bottom. This drain is installed on the uphill side and around the ends of the disposal field. The purpose of the curtain drain is to intercept and divert ground and/or surface water around the disposal area. See Illustration 5-4.

CURTAIN DRAIN
ILLUSTRATION 5-4

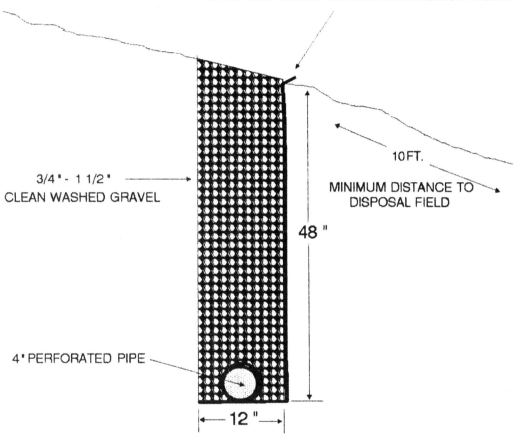

PLASTIC LINER PLACED AT BOTTOM AND DOWNHILL SIDE OF TRENCH

3/4" - 1 1/2"
CLEAN WASHED GRAVEL

10 FT.

MINIMUM DISTANCE TO
DISPOSAL FIELD

48 "

4" PERFORATED PIPE

12 "

In the section of curtain drain above the drainfield the minimum fall
is 6 inches per 100 feet.
The outlet should end below the lowest leach line.
The outlet opening should be covered with a screen.

SAND-FILTER SYSTEMS

Sand-filter systems may be required for a variety of reasons. These systems can be expensive, but in many cases are the only type of sewage disposal approved. Liquids are discharged from the septic tank to the sand filter, then through the sand filter and on to the disposal field. Due to the sand's filtering efficiency, ground water and soil requirements are not as stringent as with standard systems. Required set-back distances from water sources and drain field length are sometimes less than those of standard systems. When faced with limited space for initial and/or repair areas, sand filters may be the solution.

Sand-filter systems are large filters, some twenty feet by twenty feet and four feet in depth; for distribution there is also a one-foot layer of drain rock on top surrounding a series of perforated pipes in the middle. Underneath is a two-foot layer of sand for effluent to filter through, then another one-foot layer of drain rock at the bottom, with a perforated pipe placed at the bottom for collection and distribution to the disposal field. Distribution pipes at the top require enough pressure to evenly distribute effluent over the top of the filter. In most cases this requires a pump system from the septic tank. There must be at least a twelve-foot elevation drop between septic tank and sand filter to eliminate the need for a pump. If working against gravity, a second pump may be required to transport effluent from the sand filter to the disposal field. These factors create a wide price range.

ENGINEERED FILL SYSTEMS

When sanitation approval is denied, an engineered fill system may be the last resort. These systems require time and money to complete. The area must be large enough for the initial disposal field as well as a replacement disposal field. These systems require an area approximately 150 feet long, 70 feet wide and filled to a depth of four feet. 2,000 to 2,500 cubic yards of soil are needed to construct an engineered fill. The distance the fill material must be hauled is a major cost factor. Even with a short haul, an engineered fill without a septic system installed could cost more than a complete sand-filter system.

The engineered fill design and the soil must meet approval prior to construction. Compaction is very important during the construction process. Once constructed, the fill must sit for one year, after which test holes are dug before approval is granted.

CHAPTER SIX

Developing Access And The Homesite On Raw Land

Purchasing bare land is not to be feared. You just need to understand what is involved in development.

Creating access is usually one of the highest priorities for a new owner. Poor road systems burden everything else you attempt to do. Once there is good and solid access, it becomes easier to accomplish further development.

EASEMENTS AND RIGHTS-OF-WAY

All easements or rights-of-way of record that cross your parcel are described in the preliminary title report and are set out in your title insurance policy. Make sure you have an accurate understanding of all easements or rights-of-way that cross your land for the use of others and all easements or rights-of-way that give you access or services.

Easements are created to grant access to one party across another party's land. An easement is an interest in land owned by another that entitles the easement holder to specific, limited use.

Rights-of-way are legal rights of passage over another person's ground. Easements include uses such as ingress and egress. This type of easement allows a neighbor to cross your property to get to his. Perhaps your neighbor has not yet developed his parcel. You need to determine if there will be one or two driveways on your land to accommodate both parcels. If only one driveway is needed, perhaps you can share the cost of the driveway across your land with the party involved.

As land is divided into smaller parcels for sale, access to all parcels for sale is usually designed to be as efficient as possible. In many cases, the access road is laid out first, then lot lines drawn to accommodate placement of the road. As land is developed, roads are built, making all the saleable parcels accessible. This may result in easements across some parcels to benefit all others whose parcels lie beyond that point. The developer may have reserved easements over some individual parcels to create access to other parcels behind. Easements typically have precise legal descriptions showing the exact place in which the easement must occur. This may limit your choices for locating your driveway or other improvement. The former owner may have divided the parcel, granting an easement across the land you are purchasing. The owner of another parcel may have an easement across your property or you may have an easement across someone else's parcel.

Water Line Easements

When developers sell property divided into smaller parcels, they may have developed a water source to service several parcels, reserving water line easements across the necessary parcels.

Sewer Line Easements

Sewer lines may cross private parcels, or a neighbor's septic transport line may cross your property.

Septic System Installation & Maintenance Easements

Some soil compositions make it impossible to obtain a septic system permit. Some parcels simply will not qualify. Smart developers have reserved septic system easements across selected parcels for the benefit of others to insure the marketability of all parcels. If you buy a parcel without septic system approval and then discover that the site does not meet approval standards, you may have to go begging to your new neighbors for an easement in order to install an approved septic system.

Overhead Utility Easements

Electric and telephone lines cross many parcels and the terms of the easements often restrict what can be built, planted and grown under these wires. There may be occasional maintenance performed by utility companies as well.

Easements For Access To Service Utility Lines

Even if the utilities are not on your property, the access road may be. Secure the utility company's permission before assuming you can use their road for access. To eliminate potential problems, access arrangements should be made prior to closing the real estate transaction.

Underground Utility Easements

Easements may allow underground gas lines, sewer lines, telephone lines, electric power lines or water lines to cross your property. Damage occurs when land owners do not know exactly where buried lines are. If there is an underground easement across your parcel, it is recommended that you determine exactly where the utility is and mark it well. If, while putting in your water line you cut the phone line that serves 50 or so of your neighbors, it could ruin your day. It will ruin another day when the repair bill from the phone company arrives! Many counties offer utility locating services organized by area utility companies to provide exact locations of underground utilities. The golden rule is *CALL BEFORE YOU DIG!*

Forest Service and Bureau of Land Management Easements

There are millions of acres of public land managed by these agencies. With many parcels requiring access, Forest Service and BLM roads cross many private ownerships. These roads are often open to the public and can get hectic during hunting season. They may also be used by logging trucks, heavy equipment and service vehicles. If you hope to use the existing road for all or part of your driveway, be sure to get written permission from the agency involved. The time to answer these questions is before closing the real estate transaction.

THE BASICS OF DRIVEWAY CONSTRUCTION

Start with excavation of the road bed, including culvert installation to ensure proper drainage. Add base rock to the desired width and depth, complete with finish rock, compacting and grading.

WHERE TO PUT THE DRIVEWAY

You may have two or more choices for driveway locations. Here are several things to consider:

DISTANCE TO HOMESITE

Although the shortest distance between two points is a straight line, a straight line is not always the best way to build a driveway. The homesite may be 1,000 feet from the county road, but too steep (in excess of 15% grade) for comfortable daily use. The length of this driveway could be 1,500 to 2,500 feet.

Most people consider cost to be the dominant influence upon driveway decisions. Length is the largest factor in construction costs. Depth of rock and width of the driveway also have major effects on overall costs.

TOPOGRAPHY

The land's shape and steepness are referred to as the topography. Any driveway or road construction takes topography into account. Grades of 15% or greater are too steep for everyday homesite use. Cement trucks, dump trucks, delivery trucks, moving vans and friends may incur traction difficulties caused by driveway steepness. Maintenance costs on steep gravel driveways are higher than level drives. Vehicles lose traction as they ascend, displacing gravel and destroying the road's integrity. Compacting steep driveways by watering with a water truck and rolling with a vibrating roller will add to its integrity. Asphalting, although expensive, makes a steep driveway very usable and attractive while keeping maintenance costs to a minimum.

When laying out your new road, work with the topography. This does not necessarily limit you to only one choice. Ultimately, the driveway must shed water to one or both sides. Depending on the topography, drainage methods vary. See Illustrations 6-1 and 6-2.

The following three examples work with the existing topography to produce a driveway that does not exceed 10% in grade.

TYPICAL ROAD
CONSTRUCTION

ILLUSTRATION 6-1

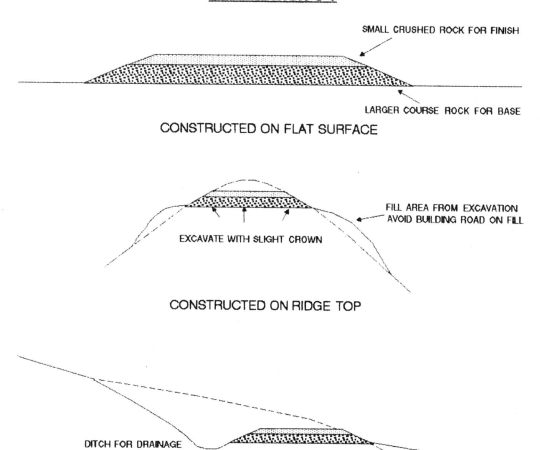

SMALL CRUSHED ROCK FOR FINISH

LARGER COURSE ROCK FOR BASE

CONSTRUCTED ON FLAT SURFACE

FILL AREA FROM EXCAVATION
AVOID BUILDING ROAD ON FILL

EXCAVATE WITH SLIGHT CROWN

CONSTRUCTED ON RIDGE TOP

DITCH FOR DRAINAGE

FILL AREA

CUT AND FILL / SIDE HILL

TYPICAL ROAD CONSTRUCTION

ILLUSTRATION 6-2

COMPACT FILL AREA OR ALLOW FOR SETTLING

FOR THE LIMITED USE TYPE OF ROAD
THIS MAY COST LESS TO CONSTRUCT

SIDE HILL WITH " OUTSLOPE "

SLOPED TO DITCH

BUILD ROAD WITH A SLIGHT TILT TO THE DITCH

CONSTRUCTED THROUGH A LOW AREA

ROADS BUILT THROUGH WET OR LOW AREAS WILL REQUIRE
AN ADDITIONAL LAYER OF EXTRA COURSE ROCK

In Illustration 6-3, Example One follows the ridge top and consequently has excellent drainage, keeping culvert and ditching costs to a minimum.

Example two is the shortest distance, but requires drainage ditches and culverts.

Example three is the scenic route along the creek and up around the hill to the homesite.

THREE DRIVEWAY OPTIONS

ILLUSTRATION 6-3

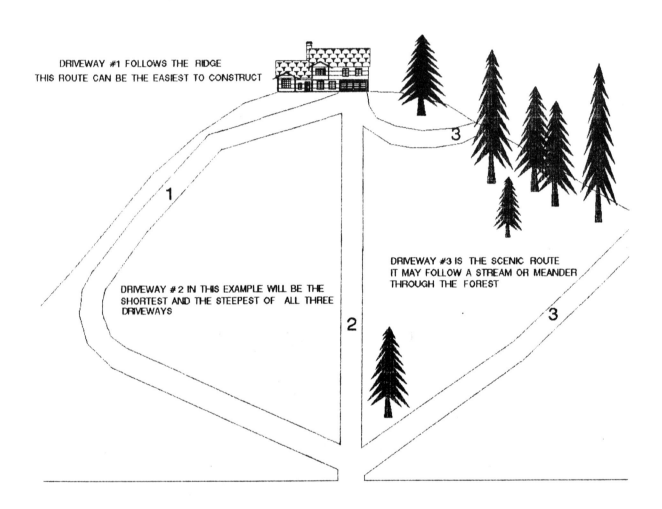

DRIVEWAY #1 FOLLOWS THE RIDGE
THIS ROUTE CAN BE THE EASIEST TO CONSTRUCT

DRIVEWAY #2 IN THIS EXAMPLE WILL BE THE
SHORTEST AND THE STEEPEST OF ALL THREE
DRIVEWAYS

DRIVEWAY #3 IS THE SCENIC ROUTE
IT MAY FOLLOW A STREAM OR MEANDER
THROUGH THE FOREST

CLEARING ACCESS (TREES, STUMPS, OR BRUSH)

Clearing light brush with a crawler tractor is very efficient and does not have much effect on the cost of the driveway. Small trees and stumps are quickly removed, but not as easily as light brush. Depending on their number, small trees and stumps have a moderate effect on the overall driveway cost. When large trees and stumps are involved, clearing costs play a major role in construction costs.

CULVERTS

Culverts are made of metal or plastic, available in many diameters and are commonly used to pass water under driveways. They usually come in twenty-foot lengths and can be joined together with collars. When using culverts, make sure the diameter you choose is capable of passing all extreme flows during the winters ahead.

Check culverts as frequently as possible, especially during the rainy season to insure the inlets remain clear. Using pipes or culverts smaller than six inches in diameter encourages nesting by rodents and other small mammals during the dry season and can clog with leaves in the fall. Screens, wire mesh and pre-manufactured guards work well if firmly attached to the culvert and kept clear of debris. Illustration 6-4 shows some culvert uses.

CULVERT USAGES

ILLUSTRATION 6-4

PLACE CULVERTS IN ALL LOW SPOTS

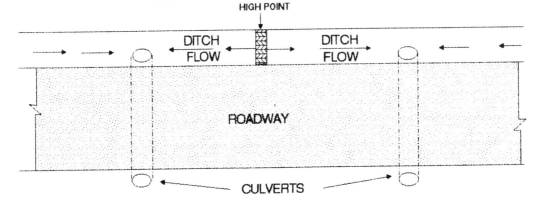

LONG STRETCHES MAY REQUIRE INTERMEDIATE CULVERTS

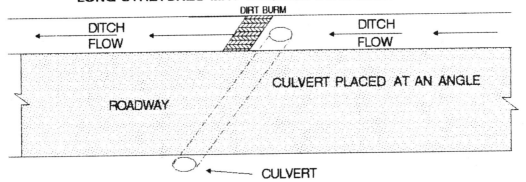

SINGLE CULVERTS MUST BE LARGE ENOUGH TO HANDLE WATER

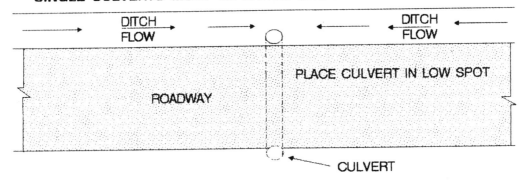

DEALING WITH WET SPOTS

When a wet area is in line with your choice of driveway location, be ready to use six-inch rock or larger. If smaller rock is used, it will disappear repeatedly and result in increased maintenance costs until properly repaired with larger rock. Attacking wet spots with large rock usually firms up the road bed and renders it more suitable for use.

As culverts are placed, give special attention to evacuating water away from wet spots.

Since most road building is done during summer, it is beneficial to take a close look for wet spots and other potential drainage problems in the winter, during heavy rains.

If the wet spot you are faced with is very large, it can play a major role in construction costs. Because of soil composition, some wet spots have little, if any, weight-bearing capabilities, requiring a substantial amount of base rock. One bad wet spot twenty feet long can necessitate as much rock as 200 feet of road on hard dry ground.

Remember, if you want trouble with driveway construction, JUST ADD WATER! It sometimes costs twice as much to build a driveway in the winter as it does in the summer. To achieve the proper stability, driveway construction requires more rock when the ground is wet and soft.

TYPE OF SOIL

Soils vary from well-drained river loam to impermeable black clay that is gooey all winter and hard as rock in summer, with long and wide cracks forming as summer dries it out. Some say that you can work black mud only one day each year, as every other day it is either too wet or too hard.

The type of soil on the parcel may not have much effect on driveway construction costs if the driveway is built during the dry season. If, however, the driveway must be built in winter, some soils require more rock than others to stabilize. Soils with the least weight-bearing capabilities are at their worst when saturated with water.

OBNOXIOUS ROCK

Obnoxious is defined as "in the way of" or "disgustingly objectionable." If you must build your driveway through rocky outcroppings, you will certainly develop other definitions as well. Road building through rock requires a large crawler tractor or an excavator (a large hydraulic shovel), a jackhammer and compressor or dynamite to loosen rock for removal. Depending on the distance of the rocky area, a lot of money can be spent getting through these troublesome spots.

Some rocky outcroppings are easier to deal with than others, depending on hardness and structure. If the rock is fractured throughout, it may move relatively easily and even benefit the road construction project. If, however, the rock is hard and solid, you may want to select another location.

ROAD BUILDING MATERIALS

SHALE

Rock formed by the consolidation of clay, mud or silt is called shale. Available at most commercial quarries, shale is cheaper than harder rock that must be run through crushers. A crawler tractor or excavator simply scoops the soft rock out of the hillside and loads it into waiting dump trucks. You may have a potential shale pit on your property which can greatly reduce overall driveway construction costs. It may benefit you to meet your new neighbors and inquire as to the location of the nearest shale pit.

Shale is normally good only for base rock and must be covered with finish rock to seal it against the elements. When exposed to air and water, shale breaks down quickly, diminishing its weight-bearing capabilities and may not support the weight of a vehicle. Once covered with quality crushed rock, shale makes a good base. Because of its low cost, it can be used in high volumes when dealing with bad spots or used to raise low spots.

Shale's advantages include the facts that it is cheaper than crushed rock, is sometimes closer to your project or is on your property, and is easily produced with heavy equipment.

CRUSHED ROCK (GRAVEL)

Commercial rock quarries are in business to provide crushed rock in various sizes for use in and around the community. Since a large portion of gravel cost is in the hauling, determine which quarry is closest to your site. If you are using a local contractor, he will know where the closest usable rock is.

As the property develops, you will discover the continuing desire for more crushed rock. Here are some of the many uses for different kinds of crushed rock:

Road construction

Driveway construction

Walkways

Parking lots

Landscaping

Construction

Spring development (drain rock - no fines)

Curtain drains (drain rock - no fines)

Septic systems (drain rock - no fines)

Stream bank stabilization (rip-rap)

Hillside stabilization (rip-rap)

Once rock is dislodged from quarry walls by blasting or other means, it is ready to move to the crusher. As rock is crushed it is screened to the appropriate sizes and rides a conveyor belt to be stockpiled.

The screening process allows anything smaller than the designated opening to go through. The result is a large quantity of smaller rock and rock dust. This rock powder is called *minus* or *fines*, and is an integral part of a driveway's ability to shed water. The importance of fines cannot be over-emphasized when dealing with a steep driveway.

Rock designation normally describes the size of the screen. Here are some examples:

3/4'' to 0'', sometimes referred to as *three-quarter-inch minus*, consists of rocks ranging from 3/4'' diameter down to fines.

2'' to 0'', sometimes referred to as *two-inch minus*, consists of rocks ranging from 2'' diameter to fines.

3'' to 0'', sometimes referred to as *three-inch minus*, consists of rocks ranging from 3'' diameter to fines.

6'' to 0'', sometimes referred to as *six-inch minus*, consists of rocks ranging from 6'' diameter to fines.

PIT RUN

Rock of various sizes that has not yet been taken to the crusher is called *pit run*. Because it has not been crushed, it is usually cheaper than crushed rock. Pit run can be used to fill wet spots and raise low spots.

Crushed rock does not all come from quarries. It may be taken from a river as round river rock and then sent through the crushing process.

James R. Harris

DRAIN ROCK

Gravel that allows easy passage of water is called drain rock, and it can be made from crushed quarry rock or round river rock. Because of additional screening, it has no fines and the rocks are uniform in size. Drain rock comes in many sizes and has many uses, such as, septic systems, curtain drains and spring development. These uses all allow the underground movement of water.

Due to the absence of fines, drain rock is a poor choice for driveway construction. Because rocks are always moving under the weight of vehicles, the driveway never develops hard and water-tight integrity. This is exaggerated to such a point on steep driveways that it soon becomes intolerable.

BAR RUN

The mixture of round river rock of various sizes and sand is called bar run, and it is generally sold just as it comes out of the river.

If the closest commercial gravel operation uses river rock, you may want to consider bar run for base rock. It is usually cheaper than crushed rock and makes for an adequate base. It is not recommended for finish rock, because the rocks are round and continually move under the weight of vehicles.

HOW MUCH ROCK

Here is the formula used to determine how many cubic yards of gravel will be needed for your driveway:

LENGTH (feet) X WIDTH (feet) X DEPTH (feet) DIVIDED BY 27

As an example, a 1,000-foot driveway that is twelve feet wide and one foot deep would take 444.5 cubic yards of gravel; that is 1,000 (length) times twelve (width), times one (depth), which equals 12,000, and is then divided by 27, resulting in 444.5 cubic yards of gravel.

A 1,000-foot driveway that is twelve feet wide and six inches deep would take 223 cubic yards of gravel; that is 1,000 (length) times twelve (width), times one-half (depth), which equals 6,000, and is then divided by 27, resulting in 223 cubic yards of gravel.

A 1,000-foot driveway that is twelve feet wide and three inches deep would take 111 cubic yards of gravel; that is 1,000 (length) times twelve (width), times one-quarter (depth), which equals 3,000, and is then divided by 27, resulting in 111 cubic yards of gravel.

If you choose to compact the driveway with a vibrating roller, divide by 18 instead of 27, because the gravel will become more dense and produce less volume.

How much rock you need depends upon your site and how wet it is during the construction period. If the ground is hard and rocky you may need only three inches (1/4-foot) of finish rock. Usually, four to six inches of 3'' to 0'' base rock is topped with two to four inches of 3/4'' to 0'' or 1'' to 0'' finish rock, with wet spots and low spots receiving special attention.

PICKING THE HOMESITE

The homesite area includes the house site and the area around it that will be used for recreation, outbuildings, recreational vehicle parking or landscaping.

There may be several potential homesites on your property, making it difficult to choose the one offering the most benefits. Here are some items to consider:

Where is the approved area for the septic system?

Where does the water come from?

Where do the utilities come from?

James R. Harris

Which site offers the best access?

Which site offers the best view?

Which site offers the best drainage?

Which site is least expensive to develop?

Which site is most expensive to develop?

Most instances require a permit for the septic system before a building permit can be secured. The septic permit authorizes and designates specific locations for construction of the septic system. If the seller did not give it to you and you have not gotten it, you probably do not have approval. GET ONE SOON! Apply for a septic permit through the appropriate agency in your area. As land use rules become more stringent, septic system requirements are more difficult to meet. A parcel that might have had no problem securing a permit five years ago may not qualify today.

Once the location of the septic system has been determined, you can begin planning the homesite. Keep in mind that if you put the dwelling at a level below the level of the drain field, waste water and effluent will have to be pumped uphill to the septic tank. Properly installed, pump systems are efficient and essentially maintenance-free.

Distance to water and utilities plays a major role in homesite development costs. Many people underestimate the costs involved when bringing utilities to a homesite. You or your agent must meet with each company representative on your site to discuss options, if any. The further your homesite is from the origin of these services, the more expensive they will be to secure.

When considering homesite options, try to envision the finished project. It is always nice to have enough room for easy access to both front and rear of the finished dwelling. Try to include enough room for an outbuilding, such as a garage, shop or barn. Most rural land owners have occasional needs for excavation and gravel. This requires adequate access for dump trucks and trailers. You and your contractor will appreciate the presence of a turnaround area near the homesite.

When considering a site with obvious drainage problems, you may be asking for trouble. Through the use of curtain drains or drainage ditches many problems can be solved. However, in extreme cases, the county building department may require an expensive, engineered foundation under the house.

Most owners have the homesite area roughed-in as part of the driveway construction to make use of heavy equipment while it is on site.

Topography plays an important role in determining how much excavation must be done to create a homesite. The following illustrates different topographic and drainage configurations. These examples presume that the builder has a level, accessible and well-drained homesite area in which to construct your home. Your building contractor may want to oversee the house pad excavation. See Illustration 6-5.

By putting this information to use along with other homesite options, it may be easier to make decisions that most benefit you and your family.

TYPICAL HOMESITES

ILLUSTRATION 6-5

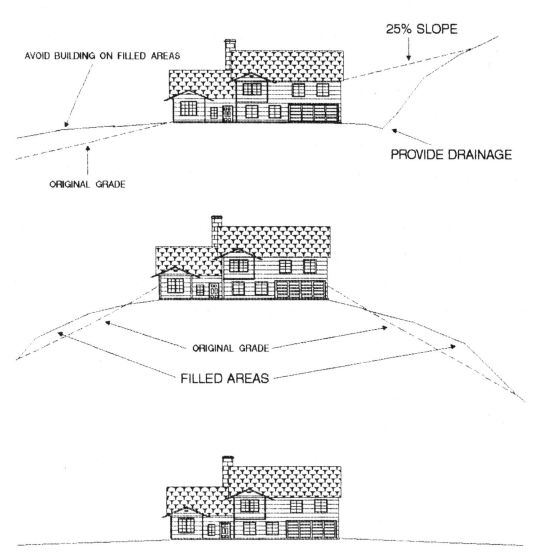

25% SLOPE

AVOID BUILDING ON FILLED AREAS

PROVIDE DRAINAGE

ORIGINAL GRADE

ORIGINAL GRADE

FILLED AREAS

BUILDING ON FLAT LAND MAY ONLY REQUIRE
EXCAVATION FOR THE FOUNDATION WITH
A SLIGHT CROWN TO ASSURE PROPER DRAINAGE

ABOUT MOBILE HOMES

Mobile homes prove to be the most sensible and inexpensive dwelling for many land owners. They can be living on their properties sooner than if they had built conventional houses. The construction time for a house could be three to six months, but a mobile home can be set up in less than three weeks.

A good, used mobile home makes an excellent residence while awaiting completion of home construction. If home construction is several years away, many prefer the double-wide mobile home, for the sake of everyone's personal space.

Two of the most valuable uses of mobile homes occur when the owner will not be able to live on the parcel for several years. First, renting the residence can provide income, maintenance and security for the absentee owner. Second, by placing a mobile home (complete with all permits) on the parcel, you secure the potential to later replace the mobile home with a conventional dwelling. I can think of several examples of individuals who were planning to build on their previously-purchased parcels after retirement, only to be saddened to find out that their parcels no longer qualified for building permits. They did qualify for building permits at the time of purchase, but due to changes in land use regulations occurring since the dates they purchased their parcels, the sites no longer qualified.

Keep in mind that some areas restrict the use of mobile homes. Protective covenants may exist allowing mobile homes only during the period of new home construction. The covenants may restrict size specifications of the mobile home as well.

James R. Harris

CHAPTER SEVEN

Can The Acreage You Are Considering Produce Income?

Not every property has the ability to earn money for its owner. If money-earning capability is an important selection consideration, the choice of parcels may be limited. Rural properties may provide supplemental income to their owners through marketing of a product or by providing food and heat that would normally be purchased elsewhere. The financial return of any income-earning capability is proportional to the amount of work put in by the owner and the product's marketability.

If looking forward to retirement and purchasing a parcel with the intent to build later, you may want to consider planting hardwoods, conifers or orchards now to enhance the potential and livability of your future ownership.

FOREST LAND

Tree farming is an excellent use of lands too steep or otherwise unfavorable for agricultural pursuits. In many cases, however, the pay-off is in the distant future. When you are considering tree-covered parcels, age, species and stand condition have a definite effect on the property's future income-producing capability.

Christmas tree farming usually begins to produce income after six years of labor-intensive work, including planting, browse proofing, repeated grass control, repeated shearing and ultimate harvesting. A well-managed Christmas tree farm illustrates the ability of a small property to provide income.

Firewood sales sometimes benefit the land owner. If the property is tree-covered and the stand needs to be thinned or cleared to enhance future use, marketing firewood may be a reasonable option. Harvesting firewood is labor-intensive work and does not always provide large net gains. It does, however, accomplish ulterior motives, such as cleaning, thinning or clearing at little or no cost to the landowner. Harvesting firewood for personal use can save up to $500.00 per year in heating costs.

Portable sawmills offer the opportunity to produce lumber from your own trees for construction of a new home or outbuildings. With enough resource, it may be possible to market your own lumber products.

AGRICULTURAL LAND

Field, seed or row crops of all descriptions can provide supplemental income, but require equipment and expertise.

Vineyards and orchards can be profitable as well, but they require careful planning and knowledge of species and market conditions. It may take five or more years of dedicated work before your labors are rewarded.

Where soil conditions and topography allow, hay production can provide income or feed personal livestock.

Livestock your property may support could include horses, cattle, sheep, pigs, goats, turkeys, chickens, rabbits, and exotic birds and mammals.

RECREATION

Your property may be situated in such a way to allow you the opportunity to charge access fees for recreational activities, including camping, fishing, photography or hunting.

Where county regulations allow, bed and breakfast inns are an enjoyable way to produce income.

ADDITIONAL INCOME SOURCES

Rock or shale pits can save thousands of dollars in development costs. If the rock or shale is suitable, leasing the pit or charging by the cubic yard for material removed is possible.

Renting or leasing mobile homes, buildings or land is a conventional method of producing income from your property. Remember, however, that any landlord will tell you it is not quite as easy as you may first expect. Screen tenants or lessees carefully and check on them and the property as frequently as necessary for your peace of mind. If you are an absentee owner, ask a neighbor to look in on the place from time to time, or consider the services of a property management company. Property management companies are in business to keep your place occupied, deal with tenants on your behalf, collect rents and deposits, then deduct their fees and send you a check for the balance.

Improving for resale can net substantial financial gains upon sale of the parcel.

All of the money-earning possibilities mentioned above require thorough research concerning the marketability of the product you intend to produce. The county extension agent is there to serve you and can provide you with valuable information. Contact any local community colleges, as they frequently offer adult education courses on subjects of interest to current and future land owners. As your knowledge increases, you better prepare yourself to make sound decisions.

CHAPTER EIGHT

Resale

In the preceding chapters we have established that any property can be improved and beautified. Certainly one of the best ways to realize income from owning property is through improving the parcel and selling for a profit.

Whether it is better road access, tree thinning, brush clearing or fencing, it would be hard to imagine any parcel not in need of some form of improvement or site beautification. The market place is very competitive and allows buyers to compare and select from available parcels within their price range. From a resale perspective, it is imperative that your parcel be appealing in as many ways as possible to attract the largest number of potential buyers. The idea of buying a parcel you can improve and resell is a good stepping stone.

Often unforeseeable changes in personal lives generate sales. This emphasizes the need to begin improvements providing the most *curb appeal* or *sizzle* to potential buyers. Start with access ways, working your way into the property via the route prospective purchasers see first. Leaving roadside areas unimproved while focusing efforts near the back of the property leaves your hard work unappreciated and unseen. As you become familiar with your parcel you will find several areas that could be improved.

When thinking of a year-round stream, people may envision a pristine, wildlife-rich riparian area. The truth is that these areas may show signs of past logging, over-grazing or other form of misuse. Stabilization can be accomplished by placing large rock (rip-rap) along damaged stream bank areas or by planting appropriate trees, shrubs and grasses to strengthen bank integrity. Stream bank stabilization ensures fewer future erosion problems. Restore these riparian areas to their highest potential.

If you are purchasing recently logged rural property, planting trees and caring for seedlings is probably the first thing to do, because it will take time for the trees to become established. These trees can be growing while you are busy making improvements in other areas. In a young forest, thinning, limbing and pruning each tree enhance the ultimate productivity of the stand as it matures.

If purchasing the remnants of a tree stand which is unusable, unattractive or unproductive, clearing and replanting is a valuable consideration. Perhaps salvaging available firewood while clearing will provide a usable resource. Replant with tree species that will provide potential income for the future owner. Proper maintenance and browse-proofing of seedlings will ensure success in this endeavor. In many states there are government-subsidized programs sharing the expense of seedlings and associated labor.

Proper pasture land management increases the livestock-carrying capacity as well as making the parcel attractive to buyers. Increasing productivity of pasture land is created by working the ground and replanting. Be careful not to allow over-grazing of improved pastures.

Improving existing road systems offers easier access to more of your property. As potential buyers consider the parcel, they will enjoy the benefits of improved accessibility. Planting fast-growing trees along the driveway is a productive way to enhance the parcel. As these trees grow they offer a certain *coming home* feeling. If you intend to keep the parcel five years or longer, planting decorative trees will put money in your pocket at time of resale.

As environmental awareness continues to grow, more and more people are buying land with wildlife-viewing in mind. Enhancing existing habitat and creating new habitat increases the numbers of wildlife species visiting the parcel in search of food, water and shelter. Real estate agents are aware that the presence of wildlife while showing a parcel has a positive effect on prospective buyers.

In many cases properties have wet areas considered unusable in the past. Once properly enhanced these wetland areas are not only beautiful, wildlife-rich areas, but attractive to potential buyers.

Keep in mind that any improvements made on the property may be added to your income tax basis, thus reducing tax liability upon resale. Keep receipts and accurate records of improvements, excavation, tree planting and equipment rental to insure that such expenditures are considered by the Internal Revenue Service.

Where finances allow, purchase a piece of equipment, make the needed improvements, then sell the equipment.

Purchasing your first parcel, improving it and later selling for a profit may begin a series of purchases and sales. The ultimate goal is for your family to live on your dream place with no debt. This is not easy and will not happen overnight. Many folks stretch finances thin when purchasing their first parcel. Subsequent purchases with these goals in mind may mean moving every five years or so.

For example, let us presume that you decide to sell your parcel to meet some financial need or merely to make a profit and move on. You may wish to enlist the services of a qualified real estate agent to facilitate this sale. If so, it may be necessary to interview several real estate agents before finding one who shares your enthusiasm for the parcel. After selecting a real estate agent, provide an information package containing pertinent information about your parcel. The package should contain the size of your parcel, its location, a description of dwellings, outbuildings and the land itself, including a description of any trees, year-round streams, ponds, secondary residences, income production qualities or other attributes. This package offers the real estate agent familiarity when discussing your parcel with potential buyers. In some cases real estate agents may think the parcel is over-priced and not marketable for quick sale.

Should you decide to market the parcel yourself without the services of a real estate agent, prepare the information package for yourself. When you advertise, the advertisement should include the property's attributes. These could include a forest, pond, year-round stream, roads and access, park-like setting, low price and good terms. As phone calls come in, give desirable facts about the property. These facts need to be real, true and accurate. The price also needs to reflect some accuracy about how much the property is worth compared to other properties in the area. A licensed real estate appraiser can provide you an accurate appraisal of value based on properties comparable to your own. When interacting with potential buyers, walk the property, letting your enthusiasm show to the buyers. You may have to interact with several potential buyers before finding one who appreciates the parcel as you do. Be prepared to answer specific questions. The buyer will be interested in all the things about the property that you were when you bought it originally. Improvements increase the productivity of the parcel, giving the potential buyer something to look forward to during his or her ownership.

Once a buyer decides to purchase, the earnest money receipt should be prepared (see Chapter Three). When filling out the earnest money receipt, ask for enough earnest money to make you comfortable that the sale will proceed. With respect to down payment, be sure to ask for an amount that meets your immediate cash needs. At this point you may want to consider such things as the amount of a down payment on the next property you may want to purchase. Since a potential sale will tie up the property and keep it off the market, make it clear to the buyer that if the sale should fail, the earnest money is non-refundable. Once this transaction enters escrow at the title company, you must wait until closing before receiving any monies. This period is a good time to be looking for your next place. Armed with experience, search for a new place needing repairs falling in line with your capabilities. And so the chain of events begins again.

GLOSSARY

ABSENTEE OWNER

An owner who does not live on the property.

ASSESSED VALUE

The value placed on a parcel by the county tax assessor for tax purposes.

EFFLUENT

Waste material discharged into the environment.

ESTUARY

The wide mouth of a river where the tide meets the currents.

FLOOD PLAIN

Level land that may be submerged by flood waters.

FORECLOSURE

A legal proceeding brought by a lender or seller to extinguish the rights of a borrower or purchaser in a certain parcel of land.

FREE AND CLEAR

Property paid for in full.

HIGH WATER LINE

The highest point on the river bank that water has reached in the last 100 years.

James R. Harris

INCOME STREAM

A flow of income derived from the sale of property.

LEGAL DESCRIPTION

Exactly describes a parcel of land.

MARSH

A tract of low and very wet land; a swamp.

ON-SITE

Carried out or located on your property.

PERFORMANCE BOND

An obligation made binding by a potential forfeiture of money.

PROTECTIVE COVENANTS

Rules and guidelines designed to protect all subdivision owners against undesirable land uses within the subdivision.

RAW LAND

Undeveloped, bare land.

REPAIR AREAS

Approved area for installation of septic system upon failure of primary system.

RESPONSE TIME

Number of minutes it takes fire department to respond to an emergency.

RIPARIAN ZONE

Relating to the bank of a natural watercourse, such as a river or lake.

STEWARDSHIP

Responsibility to manage property.

DIVISIBLE

Offers the potential under governmental regulations to divide a parcel into smaller parcels.

WELL RECORDS

History of well drilling results.

WETLAND

A parcel of land with soil that is moist and spongy, as a swamp or marsh.

Rural Acreage: *Finding The Right Place*

PROPERTY SELECTION WORKSHEET

1.   How much are the annual taxes?

2.   Are there any tax exemptions?

      Farm _____   Forest _____

3.   Are there any easements across this property?

      Yes _____   No _____

      If yes, describe _____

      _____

4.   Is the parcel dependent on easements of any kind across

      neighboring parcels?

      Yes _____   No _____

      If yes, describe _____

      _____

5.   Are there any protective covenants? (Show me.)

6.   Where is the septic system or the approved site?

      If site is not approved, why? _____

7.   Where are the property corners? (Show me.)

8.   Where does the water come from? (Show me.)

9. Where do the power and telephone lines come from? (Show me.)

10. How is the property zoned? _____

11. How are the neighbors?

12. Is the property fenced? What is the condition of the existing fence?

13. Can this parcel be subdivided?

14. Can two or more dwellings be legally placed on property?

15. What projected future uses affect this parcel?

16. What is the status of water and mineral rights?

ACREAGE _____   PRICE _____

DIMENSIONS _____   EARNEST MONEY _____

TYPE OF SOIL _____   DOWN PAYMENT _____

TERMS OF SALE:

_____

_____

_____

_____

PROPERTY DEVELOPMENT WORKSHEET

PRICE OF PROPERTY	$_____
WATER DEVELOPMENT	
Well	$_____
Spring	$_____
Water District	$_____
Municipal	$_____
Other	$_____
DRIVEWAY/ACCESS	
Culverts	$_____
Bridge	$_____
Driveway	$_____
SEWER	
Hook-up	$_____
Installation	$_____
SEPTIC SYSTEM	
Standard	$_____
Sand filter	$_____
Engineering/permits	$_____
Capping fill	$_____
Engineered fill	$_____
Pump	$_____
Other installation costs	$_____

HOMESITE EXCAVATION

Homesite $_____

Tree/stump removal $_____

Rock removal $_____

Drainage $_____

Pond/spring development $_____

UTILITIES

Overhead power $_____

Underground power $_____

Utility fees $_____

Telephone $_____

Water $_____

Natural gas $_____

OTHER COSTS

_____ $_____

_____ $_____

_____ $_____

_____ $_____

TOTAL DEVELOPMENT COSTS $_____

NOTES

NOTES

PROPERTY SELECTION WORKSHEET

1.   How much are the annual taxes?

2.   Are there any tax exemptions?

      Farm _____   Forest _____

3.   Are there any easements across this property?

      Yes _____   No _____

      If yes, describe _____

      _____

4.   Is the parcel dependent on easements of any kind across

      neighboring parcels?

      Yes _____   No _____

      If yes, describe _____

      _____

5.   Are there any protective covenants? (Show me.)

6.   Where is the septic system or the approved site?

      If site is not approved, why? _____

7.   Where are the property corners? (Show me.)

8.   Where does the water come from? (Show me.)

9. Where do the power and telephone lines come from? (Show me.)

10. How is the property zoned? _____

11. How are the neighbors?

12. Is the property fenced? What is the condition of the existing fence?

13. Can this parcel be subdivided?

14. Can two or more dwellings be legally placed on property?

15. What projected future uses affect this parcel?

16. What is the status of water and mineral rights?

ACREAGE _____   PRICE _____

DIMENSIONS _____   EARNEST MONEY _____

TYPE OF SOIL _____   DOWN PAYMENT _____

TERMS OF SALE:

_____

_____

_____

_____

James R. Harris

HOMESITE EXCAVATION

Homesite $_____

Tree/stump removal $_____

Rock removal $_____

Drainage $_____

Pond/spring development $_____

UTILITIES

Overhead power $_____

Underground power $_____

Utility fees $_____

Telephone $_____

Water $_____

Natural gas $_____

OTHER COSTS

_____ $_____

_____ $_____

_____ $_____

_____ $_____

TOTAL DEVELOPMENT COSTS $_____

PROPERTY DEVELOPMENT WORKSHEET

PRICE OF PROPERTY $_____

WATER DEVELOPMENT

    Well $_____

    Spring $_____

    Water District $_____

    Municipal $_____

    Other $_____

DRIVEWAY/ACCESS

    Culverts $_____

    Bridge $_____

    Driveway $_____

SEWER

    Hook-up $_____

    Installation $_____

SEPTIC SYSTEM

    Standard $_____

    Sand filter $_____

    Engineering/permits $_____

    Capping fill $_____

    Engineered fill $_____

    Pump $_____

    Other installation costs $_____

NOTES

To order additional copies of *Rural Acreage: Finding the Right Place*

Send $14.95 plus $3.00 shipping to:

Jim Harris
P.O. Box 898
Roseburg, Oregon 97470

2 to 4 books: $12.95 plus $3.00 shipping each book
5 or more: $10.95 plus $3.00 shipping each book

Name: _____

Address: _____

City, State, Zip: _____

Phone: _____

Quantity: _____

Total amount enclosed: _____